The Royal Wedding

THE OFFICIAL WESTMINSTER ABBEY SOUVENIR

The Royal Wedding

THE OFFICIAL WESTMINSTER ABBEY SOUVENIR

JAMES WILKINSON

University Romance

HIS ROYAL HIGHNESS Prince William of Wales – now the Duke of Cambridge – and Miss Catherine Middleton – now Her Royal Highness the Duchess of Cambridge, were married in Westminster Abbey on Friday 29 April 2011 amid huge interest worldwide. They had known each other for many years, having first met at St Andrew's University in 2001. At university they were both reading for the same degree in History of Art, though Prince William later changed to read Geography. The public knew little about their friendship until they were first pictured together on the Klosters ski slopes in June 2004.

Catherine was born on 9 January 1982, the eldest of three children. When she was two years old the family moved to Amman in Jordan where her father worked for two and a half years. Catherine attended a nursery school there from the age of three. On their return to England she attended St Andrew's School, Pangbourne, and then, in 1995, Marlborough College, a leading

British independent school, where she was successful both academically – she studied Chemistry, Biology and Art at Advanced level – and at sport. While at Marlborough she completed her Duke of Edinburgh Gold Award. Before going to university she took a year off, known as a gap year, during which she studied at the British Institute in Florence, spent some time working in Chile, and crewed on Round the World Challenge boats in the Solent. After graduating in 2005 she worked in the fashion industry, and later for her parents' firm – a party-organising business. Catherine's hobbies include sports like tennis, swimming and sailing as well as photography and painting.

Prince William was educated at Eton College where he furthered his interest in sport, captaining his house football team and taking up water polo. During his gap year he took part in Army training exercises in Belize, spent some time in Chile teaching children in the town of Tortel in the south of the country and also worked in Africa.

At university the Prince gained a good degree and also developed his sporting interests, representing the Scottish national universities' water polo team at the Celtic Nations tournament in 2004. Since leaving university Prince William has followed a military career. He was commissioned as a Lieutenant in the Blues and Royals, a regiment of the Household Cavalry, and two years later earned his wings by completing helicopter training at the Royal Air Force College, Cranwell. He has also undergone training with the Royal Navy. In 2009 he trained to become a helicopter pilot with the RAF's Search and Rescue force, and at the time of his marriage was with the Search and Rescue Training Unit at RAF Valley on Anglesey. His first rescue mission came on 2 October 2010 when he and three colleagues airlifted a seriously ill man from an oil platform off the north-west coast.

Alongside his military career Prince William has become involved in a

Left and above: Soon after their engagement was announced the couple posed for the press at St James's Palace. Catherine's engagement ring had belonged to William's mother, Diana, Princess of Wales.

number of charities, some of which reflect the interests of his late mother, Diana, Princess of Wales. He is a patron of Centrepoint, a charity assisting the homeless. In order to experience something of their plight, he once spent a night with a group of people sleeping rough near Blackfriars Bridge in London. He is also a patron of the Royal Marsden Hospital, which specializes in treating cancer, where he had spent some time doing work experience in the children's unit.

The royal couple announced their engagement on 16 November 2010. To mark the event they were photographed at St James's Palace where they gave an impromptu press conference. In their first television interview, notable for its informality, they spoke of how they met and how their friendship evolved. Asked about when he proposed, Prince William said that it was while they were on holiday, staying at a lodge on the slopes of Mount Kenya. Asked about her reaction, Catherine said it was 'a total shock', but very exciting.

Catherine's engagement ring, a blue sapphire surrounded by fourteen diamonds, had been Prince William's mother's engagement ring. Prince William said, 'I had been carrying it about in my rucksack for three weeks, and I literally would not let it go. Everywhere I went I was keeping hold of it because I knew if it disappeared I would be in a lot of trouble.'

The couple chose Westminster Abbey for their wedding, partly because of its 'staggering beauty', and also because, despite its size and its capacity congregation of 2,000, it has an intimate feel. It is an intimacy which was to be shared, through television, with many hundreds of millons of people around the world.

Left: Elegance and simplicity are the hallmarks of Catherine's beautiful dress, designed by Sarah Burton of Alexander McQueen. The lace was made by the Royal School of Needlework at Hampton Court Palace.

Right: Catherine, on the arm of her father Michael Middleton, is greeted by the Dean of Westminster before the start of the wedding ceremony.

The Wedding Day

THE MARRIAGE OF PRINCE WILLIAM and Catherine Middleton was witnessed by the largest 'congregation' ever. An estimated two billion people worldwide watched on television as Catherine, on the arm of her father, processed through the Abbey to the uplifting strains of Sir Hubert Parry's anthem 'I Was Glad', particularly fitting in the Abbey where it has been used at the start of every Coronation since that of Edward VII in 1902. Prince William and his brother, Prince Harry, had arrived at the Abbey three quarters of an hour earlier so they could greet some of their friends among the congregation before retiring to a side chapel to await the start of the service.

As Catherine walked up the nave, the world was at last able to see her wedding dress, which had been a closely guarded secret until then. It had been designed by Sarah Burton of Alexander McQueen, who also designed the dress for Catherine's sister Pippa, the Maid of Honour. The lace on the

Left: Prince William, in the uniform of a Colonel of the Irish Guards, waits at the high altar as Catherine is led through the Quire.

Above: The Maid of Honour follows with the four bridesmaids and two pages.

bride's dress was made by the Royal School of Needlework and included a rose, thistle, daffodil and shamrock – emblems of the four parts of the United Kingdom. The dress had a graceful seven-foot train. Catherine's veil was held in place by a 1936 Cartier 'halo' tiara lent to her by The Queen. Her earrings were a wedding present from her parents.

William and Catherine had chosen the traditional Anglican service as set out in the 1928 Prayer Book. The first hymn 'Guide me, O thou great Redeemer' to the tune Cwm Rhondda, gave the service a Welsh flavour – very suited to a bridegroom who is the son of The Prince of Wales. After the Dean's bidding prayer, the Archbishop of Canterbury, Dr Rowan Williams,

Left: Catherine wears a tiara made in 1936 by Cartier and lent to her by The Queen. Her earrings were a wedding present from her parents.

Above: Catherine's engagement ring is set with a blue sapphire surrounded by fourteen diamonds.

Above right: Catherine's bouquet contained lily of the valley, sweet William, hyacinth and the traditional sprig of myrtle.

Overleaf: Westminster Abbey was chosen by the couple for the ceremony partly because its 'staggering beauty' provided a magnificent backdrop for the Royal Wedding.

administered the marriage vows. First Prince William was asked if he would have Catherine to be his wedded wife. 'Wilt thou love her, comfort her, honour and keep her, in sickness and in health; and, forsaking all others, keep thee only unto her, so long as ye both shall live?' to which he answered, 'I will'. As the thousands watching outside the Abbey cheered, the noise could be heard inside the Abbey and raised a smile. Then it was Catherine's turn to make the same pledge to love, comfort, honour and keep William. Again there were cheers from outside. Prince William put the wedding ring, made of Welsh gold, on the fourth finger of Catherine's left hand with the words, 'With this ring I thee wed; with my body I thee honour; and all my wordly goods with thee I share.'

After the Archbishop had blessed the couple the hymn, popular at many weddings, 'Love divine, all loves excelling' was sung, and Catherine's brother James read the Lesson from a modern translation of St Paul's letter to the Romans, Chapter 12. It is an exhortation to live humbly and righteously: 'Bless those who persecute you; bless and do not curse them. Rejoice with those who rejoice, weep with those who weep. Live in harmony with one another; do not be haughty, but associate with the lowly; do not claim to be wiser than you are. Do not repay evil for evil, but take thought for what is noble in the sight of all. If it is possible, so far as it depends on you, live peaceably with all.'

The reading was followed by an anthem, specially commissioned for the wedding by the Dean and Chapter of Westminster from John Rutter – 'This is the day that the Lord has made', with words from the Psalms. According to the Abbey's Organist and Master of the Choristers, James O'Donnell, who

Left: (above) Prince William whispers a few discreet words to his bride; (below) the Archbishop of Canterbury, who solemnized the marriage, looks on as William places the ring on Catherine's finger.

Above: Catherine takes William as her wedded husband 'to have and to hold from this day forward… to love and to cherish, till death us do part'.

directed the music at the wedding, 'John writes in a very accessible, attractive style. His anthem is a tuneful and gentle piece and was a very good counterbalance to the bigger music with orchestral accompaniment, which was more massive in texture.'

In his Address the Bishop of London, Dr Richard Chartres, an old friend of The Prince of Wales, spoke directly to the couple, quoting St Catherine of Siena: 'Be who God meant you to be, and you will set the world on fire.' He went on, 'A spiritual life grows as love finds its centre beyond ourselves. Faithful and committed relationships offer a door into the mystery of spiritual life in which we discover this: the more we give of self, the richer we become in soul; the more we go beyond ourselves in love, the more we become our true selves and our spiritual beauty is more fully revealed.'

As the couple moved to the high altar the Choir sang a motet by the Welsh composer Paul Mealor – a setting of the words beginning *Ubi Caritas et amor, Deus ibi est* ('Where charity and love are to be found, God is there'). It is music Catherine Middleton heard and grew to like when she was at St Andrew's University. Mealor's music has been described as having 'serene beauty, fastidious craftsmanship and architectural assuredness… Music of deep spiritual searching that always asks questions, offers answers and fills the listener with hope'.

Towards the end of the service the rousing hymn 'Jerusalem' was sung, followed by the Blessing given by the Dean, the Very Reverend Dr John Hall. Now married in the sight of God, the couple, followed by their parents,

retired to the Chapel of St Edward the Confessor, behind the high altar and out of sight of the congregation, to fulfil their legal obligations by signing three Registers (two Abbey Registers and the Royal Family's own Register, which were later taken to Buckingham Palace for The Queen and certain other guests to sign). During these formalities the Choir sang another masterpiece by Parry, 'Blest Pair of Sirens'. Prince William and Catherine had taken a great deal of interest in selecting the music for the service. In December 2010 recordings were loaded onto two iPods for the couple to listen to over Christmas, and by February a final choice had been made. This was partly governed by the musical resources available: the Choirs of Westminster Abbey and the Chapel Royal, and the London Chamber Orchestra conducted by Christopher Warren-Green. Altogether twenty-seven musical works were chosen, including an hour of orchestral and organ music played while the guests assembled in the Abbey. Among the best-known pieces were Ralph Vaughan Williams' 'Fantasia on Greensleeves' and 'On Hearing the First Cuckoo in Spring' by Frederick Delius. There were also two pieces by the Master of the Queen's Music, Sir Peter Maxwell Davies.

Left: The cheers of the crowd outside can be heard in the Abbey as the couple exchange vows.

Right: The Queen and the Duke of Edinburgh, sitting at the foot of the steps, exchange a few words during the ceremony.

Left: After the Address by the Bishop of London the couple moved to the high altar and knelt for the prayers.

Above: While William looks serious, Catherine smiles broadly as they process as man and wife down through the Abbey.

Overleaf: Despite fears of rain, the weather held, allowing an open carriage procession past cheering crowds and accompanied by a division of the Household Cavalry.

The formalities over, the couple emerged from the Chapel of St Edward to a fanfare from the Royal Air Force trumpeters, directed by Wing Commander Duncan Stubbs. The fanfare, 'Valiant and Brave', had been specially composed by Wing Commander Stubbs and included the RAF 'call' in honour of Prince William, who is a serving officer. The couple processed down through the Abbey to William Walton's 'Crown Imperial', a work specially composed for the Coronation of George VI in 1937 and played again at The Queen's Coronation in 1953. As the congregation began to disperse, the organ music included Widor's famous Toccata from his Symphonie V.

At the West Gate of the Abbey the couple entered an open carriage for their processional ride back to Buckingham Palace along streets lined with thousands of cheering people. Once at the Palace the official photographs were taken, while outside the police allowed the crowd that had lined the Mall to surge forward and gather in front of the Palace to await the balcony appearance. They did not have to wait long. As the Royal Family waved, William and Catherine, responding to the shouts of the crowd, briefly kissed. It was to be pictured on most front pages the next day. The noise of the crowd was momentarily eclipsed

Left: The newly created Duke and Duchess of Cambridge look radiant as they arrive back at Buckingham Palace for the reception.

Right: Many thousands of people surged down the Mall to wait in front of the Palace for the balcony appearance (overleaf) and the now traditional kiss (pp. 32–33).

by the roar of an RAF flypast. Then the public celebrations gave way to a private party inside the Palace for 600 privileged guests.

Meanwhile at the Abbey, once the congregation had left, work started to prepare it for the influx of visitors eager to see it in its Royal Wedding setting. The floral arrangements were particularly impressive, especially the avenue of trees down the nave – a display designed by Shane Connolly, who also designed Catherine's bouquet of all-white flowers, which included sweet Williams in what was seen as a touching tribute to her bridegroom.

The months of careful preparation at the Abbey had resulted in a spectacular service, which those present will remember for years to come. The worldwide interest was, according to the Dean, a marvelous reminder that monarchy constantly renews itself and continues to be relevant and important. 'What monarchy represents is something that is not short-lived celebrity. People see in The Queen an unwavering commitment of faithful and dutiful service to God and the people. That steadfastness is immensely attractive in a world where things change so rapidly. With the Royal Family there is this extraordinary sense of continuity in service.' And of the newly married Royal couple he said, 'We are delighted for them and we wish them every happiness and blessing in their life together. It will be a life of enormous importance not only for the country but for the Commonwealth and for the wider world.'

Left: In 1947 Prince William's grandmother, now Queen Elizabeth II, married Lieutenant Philip Mountbatten in Westminster Abbey.

Right: The Queen's mother, Elizabeth Bowes-Lyon, married the Duke of York in 1923, little knowing that he would one day be King and she would be Queen.

Royal Weddings Past

THE MARRIAGE OF PRINCE WILLIAM and Catherine Middleton was the tenth royal wedding to take place in Westminster Abbey in the last 100 years. The Abbey has become the traditional place for royal weddings, though not all have taken place there. The first royal wedding known to have been celebrated there was that of King Henry I to Princess Matilda of Scotland in 1100. There were six royal weddings in Westminster Abbey in medieval times, the last one being in 1382 when King Richard II married Anne, daughter of Emperor Charles IV of Bohemia. After that there was a break of some 600 years. During this time marriages were conducted in private chapels in palaces or castles, wherever the court happened to be.

In the eighteenth and nineteenth centuries royal marriages were often arranged affairs to perpetuate dynasties, with English princes choosing their brides from the royal houses of Europe. After the Great War the Government opposed the idea of English princes marrying foreign princesses. In future, it was said, royal princes would need to choose home-grown brides.

In 1923 Prince Albert George, the Duke of York, second son of George V, married Lady Elizabeth Bowes-Lyon, the daughter of the Earl of Strathmore and the first 'commoner' to marry into the royal family for 300 years. It was a union 'encouraged' by their respective mothers, especially the Duke's mother, Queen Mary, and was celebrated in Westminster Abbey. The new Duchess of York was not to know that, following the abdication of Edward VIII in 1936, her husband would become King George VI and she would be Queen, and eventually the much-loved and long-lived Queen Mother. The bride wore a dress described by *The Times* as 'the simplest ever made' for a royal wedding, of chiffon moiré dyed to match the colour of a lace veil lent to her by Queen Mary. It seems each royal wedding at the Abbey has some unique characteristic. When Elizabeth Bowes-Lyon came to the Abbey on her wedding day she paused to pay tribute at the grave of the Unknown Warrior who had been buried in the nave just three years before, laying her bouquet on the black marble tombstone. By doing so she started a tradition followed by other royal brides – including Catherine – whose bouquets lie on the Warrior's grave after their marriage service. The 1923 wedding set another precedent when the ceremony was filmed for the first time. Gaumont Graphics copied the film at the rate of 30 prints per hour and said that by nine o'clock that evening they had produced 25 million feet of film, which was distributed around the world.

Eleven years later, in 1934, Prince George, the Duke of Kent and fourth son of George V, was married in the Abbey to the beautiful Princess Marina of Greece, reservations about marrying foreign princesses having apparently been laid aside. Princess Marina had exquisite taste and is said to have been

The Queen's sister, Princess Margaret, in a dress designed by Norman Hartnell, married Antony Armstrong-Jones in the Abbey on 6 May 1960.

In April 1963 Princess Alexandra of Kent, youngest granddaughter of King George V, married the Honourable Angus Ogilvy, the son of the 12th Earl of Airlie. Twelve-year-old Princess Anne was chief bridesmaid.

the first royal bride to become a fashion icon. Her dress, designed by the couturier Captain Edward Molyneux, was made only two weeks before the wedding. It was close fitting with a high neckline and a four-and-a-half yard train lined with silver lamé. Princess Marina's wedding made history because it was the first to be broadcast on radio by the BBC – its most ambitious outside broadcast to date – though, because it was a sacred service, there was no commentary from the Abbey itself.

The present Queen's wedding in the Abbey in November 1947 took place just two years after the end of the Second World War. Britain was going through very hard times with food shortages and rationing, so the wedding itself was especially important in setting a new agenda and helping people to look forward to better times ahead. Winston Churchill called the occasion 'a flash of colour on the hard road we travel'. The young Princess Elizabeth had chosen as her husband a handsome Royal Navy Lieutenant, Prince Philip of Greece, whom she had first met when she was just thirteen. In March 1947 he renounced his titles and adopted the surname Mountbatten from his British maternal grandparents. In September 1947 he was received into the Church of England in a ceremony at the Chapel at Lambeth Palace.

Princess Elizabeth's wedding dress, for which the Government gave 200 extra clothing coupons, included 10,000 pearls, which the designer Norman Hartnell had to get from America. Such was the intense interest in the design that photographers offered the landlord of the pub opposite Hartnell's workshop large sums of money to allow them into his rooms so they could peer through the windows hoping to glimpse the fabric. In the end Hartnell had to whitewash the windows of his studio. Searching for inspiration, Hartnell saw a picture by Botticelli, *Primavera*, which gave him his idea. The dress had a fitted bodice and a neckline with a deep scalloped edge. It had a

15-foot train, heavily embroidered with flowers including roses, orange blossom and jasmine.

The sacred part of the ceremony over, the royal couple went into St Edward's Chapel behind the high altar to sign the Register. According to a contemporary account the Princess's parents were on the verge of tears. The King told the Archbishop, 'It is a far more moving thing to give your daughter away than to be married yourself.' The Archbishop and the Dean of Westminster kissed the bride's hand, and the royal couple emerged from the Chapel to the sound of Mendelssohn's 'Wedding March'. Outside the Abbey they were greeted by a peal of bells and the roar of the crowd.

The Queen's sister Princess Margaret married in 1960, again in a dress by Norman Hartnell, though this time, in marked contrast to Princess Elizabeth's dress, it was very simple with a fitted bodice, a V-neck and a flared skirt of twelve panels. Once again there was worldwide interest. It was only the second time television cameras had been in the Abbey (the first being for the Coronation). Recordings of the television pictures were rushed to the USA and Canada by Vulcan bomber.

In 1963 Princess Alexandra was married to the Honourable Angus Ogilvy in the Abbey in another stunning ceremony. She arrived at the Abbey in a Rolls Royce rather than a coach – a pattern repeated by Prince William's bride in 2011. Her dress, designed by John Cavanagh, was of white tulle over which was magnolia lace. Her 21-foot train fell from her headdress, and she wore her mother's diamond-fringe tiara. There were four small bridesmaids in the

Princess Anne, only daughter of The Queen, with her new husband, Captain Mark Phillips, wave to the crowds from the Buckingham Palace balcony on their wedding day, 4 November 1973.

charge of the chief bridesmaid, twelve-year old Princess Anne, and two kilted pages.

Ten years later, in 1973, Princess Anne herself was married in the Abbey to Captain Mark Phillips. She had specifically requested a simple ceremony. It took place at a time of industrial unrest in the coal and electricity industries, and once again they were difficult times. Even so there was still much traditional royal splendour. It was the first time colour television had been used in the Abbey, and this added to the glamour of the occasion.

In 1986, Prince Andrew, The Queen's second eldest son, married Miss Sarah Ferguson. Perhaps the biggest impact at this ceremony was made by the floral display in the Abbey. Forty-five flower arrangers worked for several days to transform the Abbey, and after the wedding 52,000 people queued to see the flowers.

The wedding of Prince William and Catherine Middleton, though celebrated again during a time of economic restraint, will long be remembered for its glamour and spectacle, and perhaps also for celebrating the role of marriage in an age when so many couples forego marriage in favour of more informal and secular arrangements.

Prince Andrew, Duke of York, the second son of The Queen, married Miss Sarah Ferguson at the Abbey in July 1986.

After the excitement of the wedding, the carriage procession, the glittering reception, the balcony appearance and the international headlines, the Duke and Duchess of Cambridge are now living like many thousands of other newlyweds. They have made their home in a small cottage somewhere in North Wales. Though increasingly the Prince's royal duties will dictate a higher profile, the couple can at least start their married life in rural privacy.

© Scala Publishers Ltd, 2011
Text © Westminster Abbey Enterprises Ltd, 2011
Photography © Press Association, 2011, except for the following:
p. 16 © AP Images; p. 13 © Jon Bond / The Sun; back cover © Hugo
Burnand / St James's Palace; p. 7 © Corbis Images, 2011; pp. 5, 6, 8
(above right), 10, 11, 26 (above, below), 29, 34, 36–38, 40 © Getty
Images, 2011; p. 28 © James Glossop / The Times; front cover ©
Heathcliff O'Malley, 2011; pp. 12, 27 © Paul Rogers / The Times;
pp. 18, 19, 24 © Clara Molden / The Daily Telegraph

First published in 2011 by
Scala Publishers Ltd
Northburgh House
10 Northburgh Street
London EC1V OAT, UK
www.scalapublishers.com

ISBN 978-1-85759-724-0

Text: James Wilkinson
Editor: Esme West
Designer: Nigel Soper
Printed and bound in the UK

10 9 8 7 6 5 4 3 2 1

British Library Cataloguing
in Publication Data
A catalogue record for this book is
available from the British Library